HARRY IN AN AMAZING WORLD.

LEGENDS LEAGUE-BOOK 1

PRAM

This book specially designed to all the youngsters and I dedicate this book to all the childrens of the world and am so thank ful to all who supportted me through this amazing journey.

Contents

Prologue

HARRY IN AN AMAZING WORLD...

In a certain pace there lived a boy named Harry. He likes to read mysteries and amazing stories. So he likes to touch and talk to amazing creatures.

So one day when he was sleeping in his dream he saw that he is entering to an amazing world. And he was talking with some amazing creatures. He got up at once and said his father about the dream but father said this happens because you read too much of story books. But he couldn't forget this dream.

So he went to a library to relax his mind. There was a book with its cover colored silver. He opened it and that said "Do not wear this chain".

Then he thought this story will be amazing and when opened the next page of the book there was a silver chain.

He wored it at once and the whole world stopped, and an orange light displayed and through which there was a door. When he entered through the orange light, the door became into a tree. Bottom of the tree there was a small door through which a mouse could enter. He ran around the tree, but there wasn't any change incurred. Then he saw a gold key kept to be rolled into the tree.

And from somewhere a voice spoke as "You had entered the Amazing world". Then he was a bit frightened. He turned every side but he saw no-one was standing. He saw a horse was standing far away.

He ran near the horse and touched it but when it turned its front half was a human look and back half was as a horse. Then Harry asked as "Can you speak horse-human".

Then he answered that his name is "Biln" and not Horse-human. Then Harry asked the Biln about the place and Biln details. Biln said that his father looks same like him and his mother was a human. And he asked from Harry "How did you come to our world".

Then Harry said about the book and the chain. On their way, they saw a mouse with a sword was fighting with a fox. Then Biln took his secret weapon a bow and arrow, he targeted it to the fox, and then the fox got wounded and died. After then the mouse was free.

This mouse was one of the army in the palace. Biln and Harry laughed when they heard this. Harry asked from the mouse, "Where is the palace? Where are the king and the queen?"

Mouse answered to the questions as "This is the city of Amazing world and the king is in the centre of this city".

On their way, they saw an Ox, whom seems to be looking like an Ox but works and stands like a man. He also had a weapon and that is an Axe. He was as black as a crow, but was strong and also was able to speak. They felt tired after travelling for a long mile and Harry asked from the ox,

" Whether is there any place to take some rest. Then the ox spoke that "There's a place but I'm not sure that will it be comfortable to you". "I don't won't any comfortability I just need a place to sleep and that's it". On the next day Harry discovered the whole city with best friend Biln.

On their way to ox's home they met and old man who was alone. Biln carried the old man in his back. They gave food for him to consume, this man can say the future about anyone by just pointing towards the person.

Likewise this man point at Harry and said "When you touch me something is coming into my mind, so if you are in a danger soon run towards any place you get."

"When I touched you I saw a 12 headed dragon, and you have a sword in your hand."

Harry said "No sir you have mistaken I'm not the person you think I can't even carry a 2kg of rice, so how could I carry a sword."

The man said" The future will change you according to the situation. Then Harry and the mouse decided to go to the house where every old books are kept. Harry opened a book named "Savior of Amazing world".

He started to read the books for a long period of time. After that he found his name was written, that a boy would come to save the Amazing world, and that his name is Harry. While so a small wrapped paper fell down from the book. He opened it and saw, through which he saw his past, present and the future. Then he thought that what the old man had said was so true.

Later they went home and they saw that every one of their friends were ready for a war and looked as a gang of soldiers.

They all like to fight with someone but Harry said that "First, we had to meet the king and say what's going around and the war which is coming so soon."

In the palace Harry started the reason of coming to the palace by saying as," Your majesty I have a news to say you sir."

The king commands him to say what it is and Harry once again started as "Your majesty a 2 headed dragon is coming so soon to destroy this Amazing world."

We must inform this to all citizens. The king said "If this dragon story was lye you and your friends will be put for rest of your lives in the prison."

He said "I agree my majesty."And the king saw the mouse soldier and asked," How did you come once again to the palace and when did you come? I thought that we had lost you and that's a huge loss to our country."

The mouse answered as "He is Harry and I came with him and he saved my life from a fox and I came just now with them."

We came to the palace to say this and our friends are waiting for us until we come and he said mouse that they time has come for them to leave the palace. Sooner the king spoke as," You both must have come from a faraway place so come let's have some food. Mouse went to call his other friends while Harry and king were eating and the king said,

"You may stay in the palace for few days and start your work." After 2 weeks it was their time to go to their home. But as they said the 12 headed dragon hasn't come.

The king turned angry over them and he said his soldiers to bring them sooner to the palace and make them their prisoners.

As the king said the soldiers to catch them and made them as prisoners. In the prison Harry met many different prisoners. He first saw a special creature that was like a gum. He was put into a glass box, and also they saw two pumpkin sized ogres. Harry didn't know why they were been imprisoned but he knew that the king has a plan of keeping all of them as prisoners.

The way how the king kill the prisoners, was that the prisoners should have to fight against the soldiers of the palace. So from each prison they used to take one, likewise this time it was the old man who came with harry has to face the battle. He was killed by a man who could carry 10 elephants at the same time.

Same day at night, while everyone was sleeping, this man came to Harry's dream and said, "They killed me, but that's ok! You be safe and get out of this place.

Next day when he got up accidently he kicked the wall and one of the brick in the wall fell down. It was an old wall, if he just hit the wall the either sides of the wall will fall down into small pieces. So he hit the wall and Harry with his friends jumped outside the wall and escaped.

The guard of the prison came to have a look of them, but no-one was there to be seen but there was a big hole in the wall. Guard ran to say what he saw but as the guard was a fish; he couldn't walk quickly, so Harry had much time to run away from the place.

Before they escape from the prison they invited even the 2 pumpkin ogres to join with them in their escape. They ran far away and escaped from the king but they had many other troubles too such like they walked far away with hunger, fought against many wild animals. At last they got a place which looked as a small house. But it's the old palace where they found many types of weapons and some food too.

They had their daily practices there and they were trained to be fought against a 1000 men alone. As the way they fought and thought they grew stronger, intelligent, speeder and good fighters or a samurai. It was an old palace where many other kings ruled strenghtfully.

They made their own boats with wood, and kept them as their own. One day as I told about a special creature like a gum in the prison came out breaking the glass prison and started to attack the king and also made others in the palace as its slaves.

This king also had a son, who was kept secretly hidden in a room where the others didn't know. This prince saw his father was arrested as a slave, and so he escaped from the prison and on his way he saw Harry who stood as a samurai.

Prince said everyone, what happened. Harry and his friends went to fight against the gum creature, but the creature came in front by attacking them, one by one to fight with him.

First Biln went to fight, he had two weapons with him they were a sword and a bow-and-arrow. But firstly he used his sword to fight against the creature and he went on facing the fight bravely, but as his back was as a horse he couldn't jump up, so he fell for the bubble shot made by the creature.

Next so he used his secret weapon, he polished the arrow with fire and shot the creature, the creature burned and both Harry and the Ox sooner put a carpet over the fire and cleaned the floor. The king was surprised to look Harry and asked, "You said about a 12-headed dragon but this is a gum creature".

"Why was that so?" asked the king. Harry answered roughly that, "This is just the beginning, this is just one head of the 12-headed creature, and there are 11 more to come".

"Let's battle them together". Harry and his friends taught the others in the village too and made others too as samurais or warriors. Now the 12- headed dragon has only 11 heads and now it created a lion that can fly and sent it to the village.

On the day it was crated, it was sent to the village and it killed some of the villagers. At that moment Ox came in front of the lion and took his Axe to cut away the lions head.

Every one of the village thought that the lion s dead and they are free now, but the lion's neck grew once again and it beggined to fly above and attack the villagers. Sooner a pumpkin creature that was named as Rufty caught the feathers of the lion harder. The lion struggled to refrain and the next pumpkin creature named Tufty took his sword and cut down the lion's head. Rufty sooner cut it's wings and they put fire over it. It started to burn and was not to be seen.

The 12-headed dragon now got more anger and created another creature which looked as a Bear which had fins and was able only to live under water.

So now in the village, people's were very frighten and afraid of this 12-headed dragon. But they needed to be free from this 12-headed dragon for that Harry needed some other characters with super powers.

For that the whole village divided into 5 separate groups, Where the first team was lead by Harry with 20 villagers, the next team was lead by Biln with 20 villagers, the third team was lead by the mouse where there was another 20 villagers, The Ox lead the 4th team with same amount of villagers and the last team was lead by Rufty and Tufty with also 20 villagers. All of them in their path saw 5 other characters, all other teams returned but the team lead by the Mouse didn't return.

On the third teams way they saw a character who had a flute which helps him to control the person the person he wishes to control, and so on their way return to the village they met a bear which had fins. Mouse first went to fight as he was the captain of the 3rd team, but he failed because he was shorter than the bear the bear ate him and only his sword was left below. The guy who had a flute controlled the bear and made it to spit the mouse out from its mouth, by that time the other 20 villagers killed the bear and threw it back to the jungle where a tiger lived. Mouse, The flute guy along with the 20 villagers went back to the village safe and said this incident where the 3rd head of the 12-headed dragon return in a bear's structure.

Harry was satisfied with the new skill people and his team trained them to their team. All of them were with special powers such like the first found a person with magic powers, second team with electricity power, the next with the controlling power(flute guy), fourth of them was with bubble gum power and the last team can send laser from his eyes.

Next day a huge bull came to the village breaking the walls, killing peoples. Ox went in front of the bull and the laser guy helped Ox. Laser guy's laser was red in color, so it was a help for the Ox to kill the bull. The bull turned to the red ray and sooner the Ox got his axe and cut the head of the bull away to kill it.

Then the body of the Ox dis-appeared, al the villagers stood wondering, "What happened?" Then the bull changed into one of the 12-headed dragon's head, and it now has just 8 more heads and it sent its 5th head to the village into a 3 cheetahs attached together and which could run faster than the car Bugati. The creature came to the village very fast and knocked to a big brick wall and the wall broked into pieces with no injuries to the cheetah. This creature came in front of Harry, but caught another man and ran away. Likewise it killed most of the villagers and so Bubble gum person used his bubble gum power to make it stucked. It got pasted to it and was unable run by that time mouse went to the place and cut the tail first and then went to cut the faces but saw that both its side way heads were not looking straight at Harry but the centre one does. So the mouse went slowly in front and cut the centre head, the head fell down and the whole body started to burn, all looked strange by that time for the mouse but he was not to be seen, one of the villager said that he had jumped to the lake closer and the whole village encouraged the mouse for its braveness.

The earlier 12-headed dragon has now transferred into a dragon of seven heads; it got angrier over Harry and the villagers, so this time it thought to convert one of its head into a Cobra which could grow to a size of a dinosaur.

This Cobra can also swallow 5 elephants at a time; it can also blow fire from its mouth. Finally it came to the village and begin to blow fire; the village whole over began to burn, where many of them died due to fire. At this horrible moment only one could help all of them and that was the flute guy, he came in front and started to blow his flute and the cobra was hypnotized for his tune. What he did next was to blow a heavy fire over a tree and made the cobra to fall over it. Then the tree started to burn along with the cobra and after all the large cobra transformed into a small face, that was our enemy's face.

Now the Dragon has only 6 heads left and by that time it thought, "There are some peoples there who could fight against my creative heads, so this time I'll send a person whom you all would love and at last whom you all would hate a lot.

This time the Dragon converted one of its head into a handsome and good looking man, but the only difference was that his hands were used to be like Robot hands. He was sent to the village and he began his act by crying, from far away the electric guy saw this man and came closer to ask for the matter.

Then the man begins his speech as, "There are 6 of them who are troubling me and also there some other 5 special peoples with them troubling me and no-one is there to help me."

Then the Electric guy started as, "I'll help you, you just saw me who are they and I'll smash their heads into a pie, ok! Just where are they staying now?"

The Handsome guy begin as' "I had got one of them and that's you and he slammed the electric guy to fall far away, next the man hid him inside a cave and went to destroy the rest of them.

So he gave his entry to the village as a man who is looking for a job, all the villagers treated him well and likewise the man came into the village and spent a simple life there. And later the 12-headed dragon who was now a 5 headed dragon sent a team of a dangerous insect to the village, they made the peoples in the village to die by being affected to an incredible disease. These insects came to the village and begined to spread the incredible disease whole-over the village.

Every one of them in the Harry's team fought with them but they failed to protect the villagers, but the dragon's 6th head which is currently a robotic gentleman sent around a throne ball and killed all of the incredible species. Although the dragon's insect team is destroyed, this dragon's master plan with the gentle-men is working out correctly.

Next this dragon sent out 3 of its heads together with some other small warriors for a war of capturing the Amazing world village.

These 3 creatures were as follows: 'A spider combined with a spider, A big snail who can move speeder as a Bugati car and the third creature was a blue cat who can move transparent and also the small warriors with them were some of the dead skeletal armies with some others looking the same as the before 3.

Before the war Harry and his team went to the old castle to get some weapons to battle against the out-coming creatures. On their way they heard a noise calling closer a cave as, "Help! Help!". This voice was similar to the voice of their friend the Electric-guy, so they moved the rock which was kept closen the cave and they got the weak Electric-guy outer to the palace and said him to stay relaxed. By the same time this gentle-men went to call upon his team for a perfect time to attack the palace.

As he found that Harry and his team were out from the village he sent his team to the village for a war. They destroyed many of the villagers home and killed many of the villagers. Then next they moved to the palace to capture after killing Harry and his team so the gentlemen first found the Electric-guy in the first- aid room and killed him after a great battle and next he found the magic guy and killed him too, but unfortunately Mouse saw all what was going on and slowly informed everything to Harry.

Harry thought of a plan and started to battle with the gentle-men guy and the Ox with the mouse implemented the secret plan and killed the Gentle-men guy. At the end of the war the results were too bad where only few villagers were been left and they had loosed both Electric –guy and Magic guy.

But their opponent team had no-one left and the person left was only the 12-headed dragon who is now a 2-headed dragon. After all these loss Harry came to a decision of battling the dragon alone.

Both of them were so ready to battle with each other and on a day this Dragon sent a letter informing that it needed to become the king and it is the reason behind all these threatening also said if they wish to live they are provided with a 3 months of life time to move or else they had to face a battle with him.

After all the villagers lost their sleep and on a day the old man who died before cam to Biln's dream and said, "To kill that dragon you should each of its head using your arrows and afterwards Harry should however kill to dragon by cutting down its chest and the veins in its heart, and also remember all these should be done together".

So then Biln got up and informed about it to Harry. They begginned to practice more than the others. Some of the villagers were very frighten and some were looking astonished to look how the dragon looks like. All of them practiced harder with only an aim of saving the village.

Like-wise before the war day Harry found a golden-silver sword. He just waved the sword closer a tree and it cut the tree into half. Harry got the sword and kept it polished everyday and he prepared himself for the war. And so the day for the war beginned and the 2-headed dragon came with one blowing fire and the next came blowing ice.

It looked strange and stronger with 2 swords in its hands, it destroyed many of the properties and Biln came first to the war ground and shooted some arrows it was as a pin for the dragon it just waved them off and continued its path.

All of the people in the place fought well and the war came to an interesting part, where while everyone were battling Harry was not to be found in the battle field . But later on Harry came to field flying from above towards Biln and said him to shoot two arrows to each of its heads as per his dream and that Rufty and Tufty by that time had to tie both of its legs and said Ox to throw him faster towards its chest.

Everything work-out in the same manner and so Harry came out from its chest cutting down all of its veins in its heart. And he pulled the dragon to the ground, all the villagers thought the dragon isn't dead yet but now the dragon's gone, but in the place Harry was not to be found. They searched for him and he came out from the mud pie and everyone in the place clapped for his bravery work of saving the Amazing world from the dangerous changeable 12-headed dragon.

And after some days, he found the way to get out from the Amazing world, that was to jump out from the waterfall pathway, and so he did in the same way. When he opened his eyes after jumping from the water-fall he found himself in the public library.

At once he removed his silver chain and left the book and the chain in the same place from where he got them. But he just needed to know the writers name and it was written as this book was written by Harry Jones. And the book disappeared from the place.

And his days later on passed by slower and when he grew up he started to write many story books and got more famous.

THE END.......